Payne Brain

Level 2

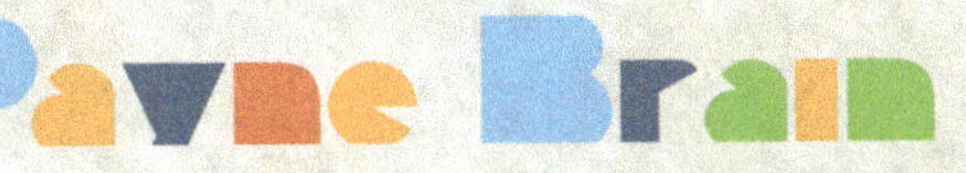

A Mister Tongue Twister Story

Ice Scream

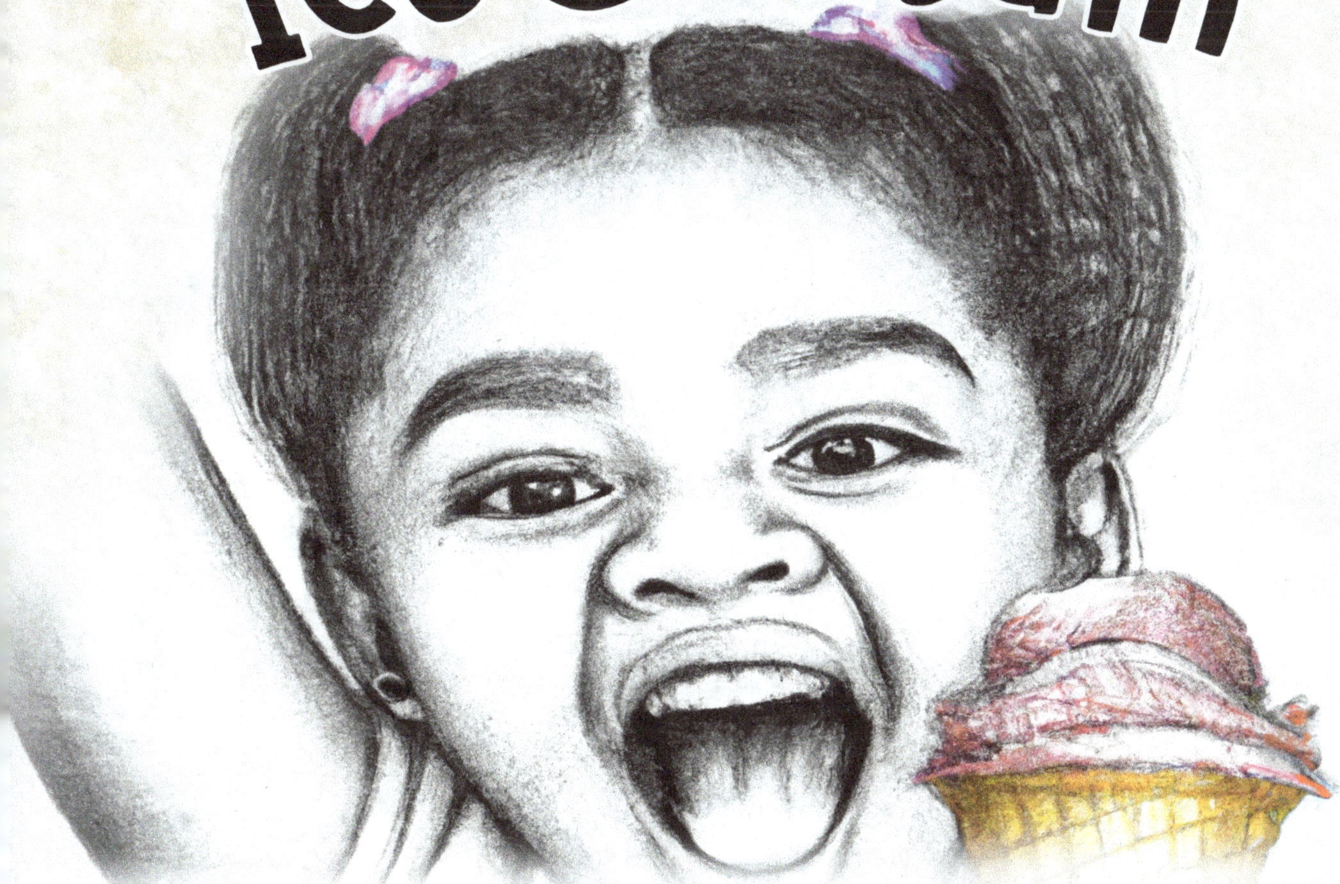

Author & Digital Artist
Carlton Payne III

To Cosima & Amarii-
Believe in yourself
-Dad

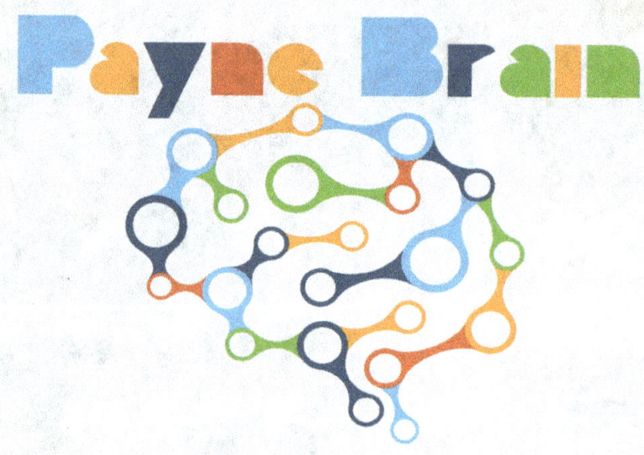

WARM-UP

I DREAM.

I SCREAM.

I'VE SEEN

ICE CREAM.

I like ice cream.

Do you **TOO**?

I like Ice cream.

I know you **DO**.

I like ice cream.

CREAMY,

DREAMY.

I think its magic,

like a **GENIE,**

I want ice **CREAM**.

I **SCREAM** ice **CREAM**.

I need ice **CREAM**.

I scream, ice **CREAM**.

I like Oreo

I like **CHOCOLATE**

Banana Cream

Rocket **SPROCKET**

Chunky Monkey

COOKIE DOUGH

French Vanilla made in SNOW

Rocky Road

Mint Chocolate **CHiP**

Birthday cake with chocolate DiP

TOFFEE COFFEE

Pumpkin **SPICE**

or cotton candy

would be **NICE**

Peanut Butter

Cheesecake QUAKE

Might make me have
a tummy ACHE.

Vanilla **BEAN**

with cream that's

GREEN

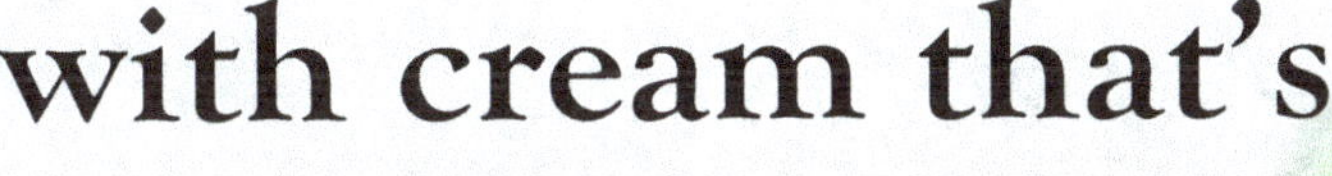

would make my tongue

a neon **SHEEN**

Cup or **WAFFLE?**

This is **AWFUL.**

Waffle bowl would be **UNLAWFUL.**

Too many FLAVORS,
waffle WAFERS.
Hot and cold
cold and HOT.
I scream Ice cream.
I scream A LOT.15

I screamed so loud

I woke my **DAD.**

That made mom

really **MAD,**

so I got sent to my room

because, I **SCREAMED**

ice **CREAM.**

I took a nap and

I dreamed Ice **CREAM.**

Maybe its my mind
playing tricks on ME .
I hear an Ice cream tune
but it couldn't BE.
Ice cream MUSIC
I might loose IT!

17

Mommy,

Mommy,

Mommy, **PLEASE**

I need Ice cream

please **AGREE**.

I need Ice CREAM.

I SCREAM Ice CREAM.

I need Ice CREAM.

I SCREAM Ice CREAM.

Mommy, says "we'll get

ice cream from the **STORE**",

but I don't want that **ANYMORE**.

I want Ice cream

from the TRUCK.

all the ice cream to EAT-UP.

I want Oreo,

I want **CHOCOLATE** ,

Banana cream,

Rocket **SPROCKET**.

 Chunky Monkey,

 Cookie **DOUGH** ,

 even Ice cream made in **SNOW**.

 Rocky road,

 Mint chocolate **CHIP**,

Birthday Cake with chocolate **DIP**.

TOFFEE COFFEE,

Pumpkin **SPICE**,

or cotton candy

would be **NICE**.

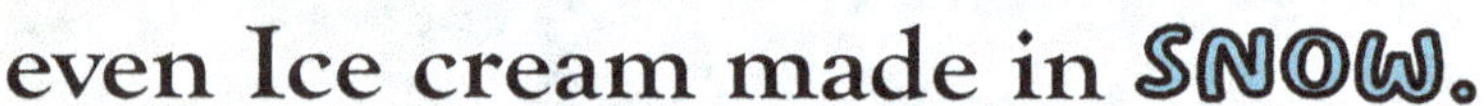
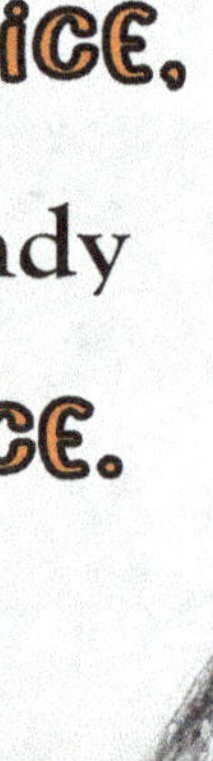
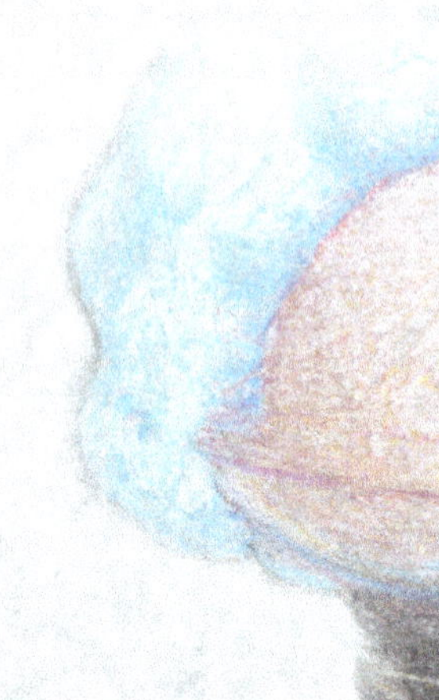

Cookies with CREAM,

The American DREAM.

Vanilla BEAN,

with cream that's GREEN,

would make my tongue

A neon SHEEN.

So many FLAVORS

and waffle WAFERS,

Hot and cold

cold and HOT,

I scream Ice cream.

I scream a LOT.

As I **SCREAMED,**

I left my **DREAM.**

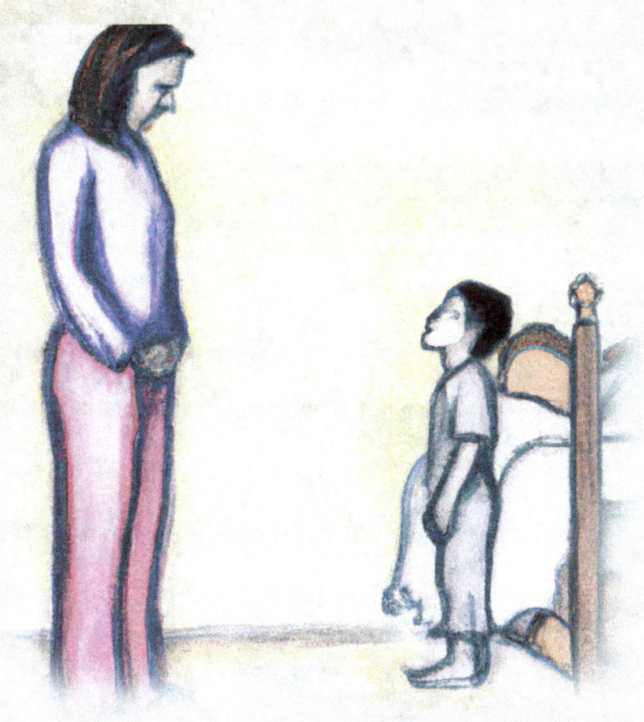

As I lay there in my **BED**,

My mom comes in and she **SAID**.

You don't get ice cream

when you **SCREAM** Ice **CREAM**.

Say please may I have Ice **CREAM**.

So if you want Oreo

or even **CHOCOLATE.**

Banana cream

or rocket **SPROCKET.**

Chunky monkey

or cookie DOUGH,

French vanilla made in SNOW?

Rocky road or

Mint chocolate CHIP,

Birthday cake with chocolate DIP,

TOFFEE COFFEE,

or pumpkin SPICE.

For cotton candy

You need to be extra NICE!

Peanut butter or

CHEESECAKE QUAKE?

You can't have that

You'll have a tummy ACHE.

Vanilla BEAN

with cream that's GREEN.

That turns your tongue a neon SHEEN!

Cup or waffle,

do you have waffle **MONEY?**

Cup it is, don't look

at me **FUNNY!**

31

So if you want Ice cream,

don't SCREAM Ice CREAM.

Say "Please can I have Ice CREAM?"

Miss Cosima Sima

Hey, Thank you for
reading my book!
Now, try to read it faster!

Oh, Have you seen my 8 mice?

34

about Mr Tongue Twister

I write rhymes

to inspire young minds

that they can be great

but it takes time.

Young or old,

old or young

You can read my stories to anyone.

Read along,

or read alone

read in the car

or at your home.

Just remember to have fun

and hopefully, you won't twist your tongue.

Hello, My Name is Carlton Payne III. I write under the pen name Mr Tongue Twister. I love to write stories incorporating hip-hop, rap, rhyming, lessons, and fun. I have many different art styles that I am well versed in, and I love to make books that look like the world that I see. I hope that you enjoy my book series as much as I did making it.

Wait, the fun isn't over.

More stories can be found on

www.mrtonguetwister.com

www.ingramcontent.com/pod-product-compliance
Lightning Source LLC
Chambersburg PA
CBHW080854160726
47999CB00009B/3118